Social Networks Manipulation

Table of contents

I'll provide social network secrets and obscure strategies that the typical user would need to spend years researching before learning.

Several companies, political organizations, and digital influencers grow their social networks (get thousands of followers quickly) using shortcuts.

I'll demonstrate how to gain thousands of followers within a month in this e-book. Prohibited and rarely revealed techniques for brandjacking, taking down the competition, etc.

Obviously, you should start by making connections and adding people you know organically (actual people), but gradually, buy followers.

I don't sure how long these websites will be up and running, however these suggestions and websites are helpful for 2023 and 2024. Additionally, this e-book may be blocked or taken down from the internet at any time, so take advantage!

Introduction

In January 2020, Instagram reported over a billion monthly users. That number is bound to go up several notches in January 2021, and this rapid increase of Instagram users only shows how far the platform has come. Currently, Instagram is a major money-making machine for businesses and social media influencers, which is why it is much more than a social media platform. Nevertheless, it is a career for many. Why should you be left behind if the most influential brands and social media influencers are making millions per post.

You have to work hard to cultivate your image on the platform before you can make money from it. There are a few things that affect how quickly and how much money you can make through Instagram.

These things include who you are, what your brand stands for, what you have to offer, and how many people trust you and turn to you for solutions. Your primary responsibility is to establish your brand's identity and ensure the quality of the products and/or services. There are ways to increase the number of your followers quickly.
Getting free Instagram followers and paying alternatives can give you

an edge over your competitors. The most important thing is to connect with your market and make a good impression.

With more followers, you will have a consistent, growing stream of people who will not only share your content, but also buy your products.

When you establish yourself in your niche and have a sufficient following, your post may appear on Instagram's Explore page.

More traffic for your blog/website: If your brand mainly works from its official website, then you'll need to use Instagram as a platform to market your website. There are many articles and blogs on the internet that recommend taking a few easy steps to fix your problem. These include including a link to your business website in your Instagram bio and all your posted images and videos.

Instagram Ads

Besides sharing photos and videos, you can also post ads to promote what you have to offer on Instagram. You can experiment with different types of ads to find the ones that work best for your brand. You can use existing content on your page and transform them into ads with the Instagram Ads feature. You must use Facebook's Ad Manager in order to create and manage ads on Instagram, as Instagram is a Facebook-owned app.

Why would you buy followers?

Is it against the rules?

Technically, it's "against" the rules, but who makes the rules? The social network itself (be it YouTube, Facebook, Twitter, or Instagram) has its own individual rules.

Suppose you recently created a YouTube channel, and you only have 40 followers. You will not be able to customize your channel link, as YouTube only allows this for channels with at least 100 subscribers.

Another example: You created a Facebook discussion group, but it only has 28 members. Nobody will easily become a member of a group that seems new or weak, not very active because they know that when they send a message, few people will see it. But if your group has 1,000 members, it will have another emotional impact, so it pays to join. It will draw in more members like a magnet.

There are two types of followers you can buy:

Fake (ghost profiles), which are bots.

Real people.

The "false" accounts are actually "bots," or software-created profiles, and their purpose is to increase the number. If you want more followers on Instagram, it will help to get suggested more on Instagram itself.

However, because they are controlled by a team and are constantly being utilized to subscribe to new channels, generate "likes," etc., these phony profiles may behave almost exactly like real ones. They often check in to the social network, making them active all the time.

As for the profiles of real people, there are sites that sell and then somehow compensate these members monetarily. I browsed websites that paid 10 cents for clicks, likes, and interactions on YouTube. For me, it was a hobby. At the end of the month, I used to accumulate $30 or $40 on PayPal, which I used for other purposes. For me, 30 dollars may be little, but for people in Pakistan or India, it becomes a lot. So it's understandable that there are membership bases for sale, clicks, and likes from real people for sale.

Fiverr.com is a well-regarded freelancer site. Gradually, it becomes a "black market", as there are already sellers who operate networks of fake profiles and sell their services. For just $10, they get you thousands of followers or likes.

Two ways to grow

You can increase your reach on social media in two ways: the hard way and the easy way. It is important to note that this does not imply that you "cheat," i.e., are lazy. I worked hard to grow my social media, but I noticed that it takes many hours a day to make invites, create connections, and interact (like, invite people, comment on posts), and after a year I only have a few hundred followers.

Do you have time after a long day at work to spend a few hours on social media? While you work hard, honestly, and slowly advance, others surpass you and develop rapidly. To you, is it just?

My recommendation is to try both methods. Continue hard and honestly to interact, advertise in search engines and directories, make blogs and write posts, invite people, interact, but at the same time give a "boost" by purchasing 200 or 300 followers.

Don't be impatient and don't buy 5,000 followers all at once! This would be a "fast" and suspicious growth on social networks; Facebook, Instagram, or any other would suspect and delete these profiles. I suggest gaining 200–300 followers and "likes" gradually over time.

Then do it organically, by yourself, through invitations from people, interactions, comments, likes, etc. Purchase 300 additional followers after a week, and so on.

If you create a website today and advertise it on search engines, it will take at least eight months for it to be indexed. It may take up to a year before you begin to see a significant increase in site traffic. Most sites no longer accept free submissions. It is necessary to pay for registration. Do you see how difficult it is?

Therefore, on the internet, there are services to buy followers, likes, backlinks, guest posts, and other methods. This is done by big brands and influencers.

If you follow the path of "honesty" and "hard work", you will fall behind. Ten years later, it might have a reasonable following (6,000 or 8,000 people), but nothing more.

The internet has become into a competitive jungle. Do you want to behave like a shark or a fish?

Websites to buy followers:

Example websites:

www.instafollowers.co

This website is reliable; it offers results within 24 hours. They accept several payment methods (except PayPal), but you can pay with Visa. It has affordable prices, for example, 1000 followers for 9 dollars, etc. As soon as you buy, you will immediately receive an email with the receipt and the progress of your transaction.
After adding followers (or likes) you will receive another email from them.

You may purchase followers on this website for several platforms, including Instagram, TikTok, YouTube, Twitter, Twitch, and Tumblr. You can also buy likes for your posts or videos. You can still buy hundreds of backlinks (links from other websites and blogs that will forward a hyperlink to your website), which are good for web positioning, traffic, and SEO.

You can also buy comments for your videos and posts.

Followers for Pinterest and repins. A repin is when a user saves your pin or tags it in their own board, helping to publicize your image "pin" post. Followers on LinkedIn.

Another such website is Famoid.

https://famoid.com/

I haven't tested it yet, but the general feedback has been positive. PayPal is accepted for payments on this website. It is said that the followers they offer are actual individuals rather than "bots". I cannot confirm whether it will be like that, but even if they are "fake" profiles,

13

they perform functions with these profiles every day because these profiles add new people every day, likes, and comments, even if managed by the same team, they perform real functions.
This site promises automatic replacement of followers on the customer's Instagram if there is a drop in their number through "automated compensation".

These websites provide followers gradually (the drip-feed method), between 1 and 2 days, so that the social network algorithm does not flag them as suspicious. These websites provide a sort of assurance: if the number of followers decreases (or some are consequently deleted), they will reimburse or add new followers (refill).

I also suggest Insta Growing, a website that is entirely dedicated to Instagram.

https://instagrowing.net/buy-instagram-followers/

They accept Visa, Apple Pay, Google Pay, and bitcoin as forms of payment. You may, for instance, spend $8 to get 500 Instagram followers. There are two types of followers for sale: the "simple" and the "premium", both with a 30-day guarantee and guaranteed replacement.

They include an innovative automated service of likes (autolikes) in which you register your Instagram and whenever you publish a new post, you will receive likes on that post in an automated way.
Their algorithm is able to identify when there is a new post on the customer's Instagram and the profiles that like it.

https://instagrowing.net/buy-instagram-autolikes/

Price for 80 autolikes starts at $19.99.

They also sell comments for Instagram.

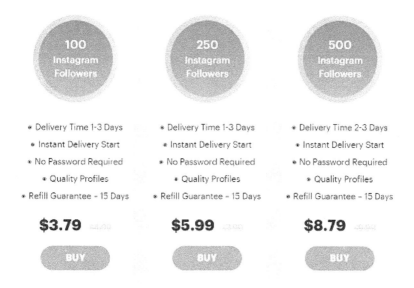

100 Instagram Followers	250 Instagram Followers	500 Instagram Followers
• Delivery Time 1-3 Days	• Delivery Time 1-3 Days	• Delivery Time 2-3 Days
• Instant Delivery Start	• Instant Delivery Start	• Instant Delivery Start
• No Password Required	• No Password Required	• No Password Required
• Quality Profiles	• Quality Profiles	• Quality Profiles
• Refill Guarantee – 15 Days	• Refill Guarantee – 15 Days	• Refill Guarantee – 15 Days
$3.79	**$5.99**	**$8.79**
BUY	BUY	BUY

The fourth website I recommend is Turbo Media.

https://www.turbomedia.io

It has various prices; you can buy 250 Instagram followers for $10. There is also a free option, in which you sign up and follow 20 profiles and make likes (it's a mutual exchange of follow-ups and likes). They accept payments with Visa and bitcoin. A positive aspect of this site is that it has real customer reviews through Trustpilot.

What is good about this website is that it sells services for multiple social networks, i.e., also for YouTube, TikTok, Spotify, Facebook, Pinterest, Twitch. For example, 250 Facebook followers cost $25. They provide a one-year refill guarantee to reload followers.

Some of these websites may be known as the SMM Panel (Social Media Marketing). You may purchase followers, likes, and views from them, and they even offer a panel with comprehensive data on your social networks. One of them is Nord Panel:

https://nordpanel.net/

Fifth website:

Popularity Bazaar is good for many services, but I use it to receive YouTube comments and likes.

They accept PayPal and the price is affordable, 50 likes for 1,79$.

https://popularitybazaar.com/youtube-likes/

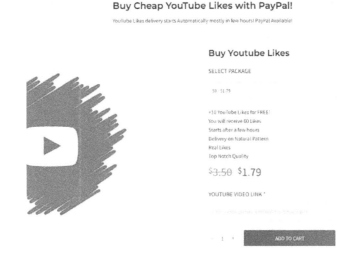

Buy Cheap YouTube Likes with PayPal!

YouTube Likes delivery starts Automatically mostly in few hours! PayPal Available!

Buy Youtube Likes

SELECT PACKAGE

50 - $1.79

+10 YouTube Likes for FREE!
You will receive 60 Likes
Starts after a few hours
Delivery on Natural Pattern
Real Likes
Top Notch Quality

~~$3.50~~ $1.79

YOUTUBE VIDEO LINK *

ADD TO CART

Others:

https://www.redsocial.com

https://promosoundgroup.net

https://www.geohits.net

In these, there is the option of real followers (real profiles) and real likes, and you may select them based on the country (geo-targeted) you like. Example: $13 for 1000 likes, $12 for 400 subscribers.

In Geohits, you can customize, for example, 200 real followers for Instagram for $2:

https://www.geohits.net/boost/instagram-followers-hq/

On this site, they accept Visa or PayPal.

https://smmlaboratory.com/facebook

SMM Laboratory also offers geolocation-based likes and followers, the ability to select the country of your choice, and low prices. They also sell traffic to websites. It offers multiple services for different social networks, such as Telegram, Soundcloud, and Spotify (for disclosing DJs and musicians), views for YouTube, followers for Discord, Dailymotion, voting on posts or polls on your website, etc. They only accept Webmoney or Visa.

Example; likes from Brazil:

https://smmlaboratory.com/facebook/fanpage/tagreted/

The Buy SEO Store offers a variety of social media platforms, as well as followers, likes, and comments for websites and blogs (Blogger). They accept PayPal and provide reasonable pricing (which is good).

https://buyseostore.com

Buy Blogger Share

$3 – $100

SELECT OPTIONS

Buy Blog Comment Backlinks

$2 – $100

SELECT OPTIONS

Social Boss

www.socialboss.org

Bitcoin or Visa are accepted. The ability to purchase followers by area is a benefit (Americans, UK, Europe, etc.). Choose premium followers (genuine, non-bot ones with established profiles and little chance of breaking or dropping).

Very important:

Never share your login or password on Fiverr or any other website where followers and likes are sold. The username and password for the relevant social network are not required for this operation; anyone who requests them from you is a fraudster.

Legality

This's "illegality" or "legality" is only a semantic distinction. Generally speaking, there is no regulation that prohibits purchasing fans and followers. The "terms of service" for each social network are what they are. For instance, if Facebook's terms of service ban the use of the word "Hitler," typing such phrase would be against the law. It just broke one of this social network's own rules; it did not break any laws.

Facebook is a little hypocritical; it prohibits ordinary users from publishing posts with links; it considers this "spam," but it allows advertisements (sponsored posts) that big brands publish about high-risk investments, bitcoin investment, and so on. Why? You know, because these ads make millions for Facebook and Zuckerberg. That is, when you pay well for something and the social network profits from it, it is no longer "illegal".

If you pay Facebook Ads itself to promote an ad, or post, to get likes, it's already legal, why? Because he's paying Facebook, Mark Zuckerberg is shoving money up his ass, so it's already legal to get likes, as long as you pay Facebook. Do you understand the irony?

Manage your own network of fake profiles

Have your own army of Facebook profiles, imagine an army of 50 or 100 profiles (realistic, verified, with friend groups, photos, addresses, etc.), with which you can do whatever you want. You can like and comment on your posts, join your group as a member, boost your publications by increasing their popularity, join groups where your original profile was banned, etc.

I'll start with the hardest part.

Account farming:

There is a methodology for "manufacturing" and "developing" networks of many accounts; one of these names is "Facebook account farming," or just "Facebook farming." This entails "developing" Facebook accounts by imitating user activity, advancing through anti-fraud screenings, account verification through SMS, and other measures. Any social network, including Twitter, WhatsApp, TikTok, etc., may be "account-farmed." Bulk accounting, which allows us to create several accounts, is another function we may employ.

There are some softwares available on the internet (no solutions in the cloud), but you must install the software on your computer. Most software requires computer experience. You may need to disable your antivirus and firewall, or make a rule to ignore the software. Windows firewall and antivirus may not allow the program to open due to potential incompatibilities, etc.

Some "bots" software costs an average of 200 dollars per year (annuity is paid); an example is the https://autobotsoft.com

Antidetect browser:

You will still have to browse the internet with an "antidetect" browser that leaves no traces of your browsing or your IP. To administer each Facebook account, it's better to use different IPs; otherwise, Facebook gets suspicious.

These browsers hide your browser's "footprints" online and change data so that there aren't many traces of what you do online.

Still, you'll need to employ dedicated proxies. I utilize "IPRoyal," a service with the "IPRoyal Proxy Manager" Google Chrome plugin, where we may purchase resident proxies for $2 each.

A proxy is a form of gateway between web servers and an internet-connected device. Web requests made from the device must go through the proxy to this provided intermediary before reaching the target web page server (e.g., Facebook). Before reaching the device, the results of the requested page first go to the proxy server, so your IP is never seen, only the proxy IP.

Some browsers for "anonymous" browsing are pricey, however "Incogniton" offers a free membership (with limited functionality) or a $29 monthly subscription.

https://incogniton.com/pricing/

Another good browser is Ads Power

https://www.adspower.com

For anonymous multilogin, it enables you to open numerous tabs in the browser (each one functioning as a separate session). It offers a limited-time free account, and premium accounts start at €9 per month (choose the monthly payment option). PayPal is accepted there.

I believe it is advisable to choose premium (quality) proxies over free alternatives.

The best way to manage multiple accounts is to use a Google Chrome extension like "IPRoyal Manager" and buy resident and fixed proxies (premium, paid, they are quality, don't use free proxies). For example, for each Portuguese Facebook account, use a specific proxy (IP) and session. For each American Facebook account, have a profile in that browser with its own IP (to pretend that each person/profile uses a different computer), understand?

Avoid "free" solutions Free VPNs and free anti-detect browsers, the free one may look "pretty" and save you money, but most use shared IPs, change IPs without warning, and your Facebook accounts will be banned because of the algorithm's mistrust.

Use quality paid services (such as anti-detection browsers, browser extensions, or proxies). "IPRoyal" has an app for smartphones.

https://iproyal.com

Dear reader, these tips that I share are valuable not just for creating and managing multiple social media accounts. Note that the internet is becoming a spying jungle as our data is not secure. Internet service providers (ISP) and companies like Google sell our data and search habits to marketing networks, we are "products".
Do you think it's fair that some websites (used for downloading movies and games) are blocked from access by internet service providers? Since you pay for internet access, you should have the freedom to visit any website you choose while keeping your data and IP safe, private, and protected. This is possible with anti-detect browsers.

In summary, for more complex "account farming", you need:

Software.

Browser anti-detect.

AND:

Proxies.

If you have a US Facebook account, use a US proxy with a US city and US IP. If administering Spanish accounts, choose a Spanish IP address, city, etc.

The Iproxy:

https://iproxy.online/

It offers IPs with geolocation and changing IPs. It is an application (App) that you install on your mobile phone, then you can choose, for example, proxies from any city and country. I'll give you an example: If you have Spanish Facebook accounts, use the application on your smartphone and access these accounts using a Spanish browser and Proxy. Iproxy has plans from $6 month.

The Proxy Store sells proxies from many countries, prices starting at $13.

https://proxy-store.com/

IP Lease is a reliable website with a variety of proxies, specially prepared to access social networks using the IPV4 protocol, with different values.

The cheapest option is to select the SMPP-1 proxy, a dedicated proxy, that costs $3 per month. Unlimited traffic. IPs from several cities in Europe and the United States. They accept payment by Visa, PayPal, and bitcoin.

https://www.iplease.io/buy-proxies/social-media-proxies.php

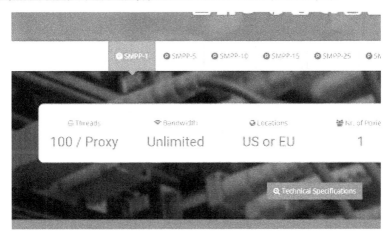

Order Summary

SMPP-1

Social Media Proxies (Dedicated)

SMPP-1	$3.00 USD
» Choose Website Usage: Facebook	$0.00 USD
» Choose Account Type: Current Account(s) Automation	$0.00 USD

Setup Fees:	$0.00 USD
Monthly:	$3.00 USD

$3.00 USD

Total Due Today

Google Chrome Extensions

Antidetect browsers for multilogin, the ability to open new tabs for social network login.

Each tab acts as a different "appliance" or different profile, with different digital footprints, so to speak.

There is a free extension for Google Chrome called Multi Login that allows you to do this; see the link:

https://chrome.google.com/webstore/detail/multilogin/ijfgglilaeakmoilpl pcjcgjaoleopfi

Includes a sample video; each time you click on the extension icon, a new tab opens, allowing you to log in to different Facebook accounts (in each tab).

When closing windows/tabs, cookies and data will be deleted from the history automatically.

Official website: https://multilogin.top

Another extension is Session Box, includes plans from $3.99 month.

https://chrome.google.com/webstore/detail/sessionbox-multi-login-to/megbklhjamjbcafknkkgmokldgolkdfig

https://sessionbox.io/plans/auto-renewal

Another extension is Sendwin

https://chrome.google.com/webstore/detail/sendwin/nbnjpdfblnfaniloeh lfjkdfclljcgfn

Official website:

https://www.send.win/pricing

There is a free plan that has certain restrictions but allows for many concurrent sessions in different browser tabs and is entirely anonymous.

However, the "Pro" plan, which offers a proxy for each session, is only $2.99 a month encrypts all internet sessions using AES-256.

Proxy Extension

WindScribe has a free plan (for proxy browsing) that allows up to 10GB of browsing. It has excellent reviews.

https://chrome.google.com/webstore/detail/windscribe-free-proxy-and/hnmpcagpplmpfojmgmnngilcnanddlhb

https://windscribe.com/vpn-for-chrome

Difference between VPNs and proxies. Both can be used.

A virtual private network (VPN) will encrypt its layer at the system level, i.e., all your internet traffic will be routed through the VPN server.

The only way to use a VPN for marketing is to do it manually. First, connect to the VPN server using the VPN client. Then open your Internet browser and log in to your social network. For each active account, proceed in this way. However, some VPNs may change IPs without prior notice. Ideally, use a browser or Google Chrome extension with resident proxies.

Benefits of social network proxies over VPNs.

With a VPN, you can divert all your traffic at the system level. So all your other apps, like Google Drive or cloud-based apps, should be disconnected and connected again once the VPN connection is working. Also, you will need to connect each account individually. I tis a tiring task to manage more than ten accounts.

On the other hand, social network proxies, due to their simplicity, can be used to connect accounts manually through a browser extension. All you need to do is "rotate" or "change" the proxies in the extension. So you don't need to divert all your traffic through the proxy server. That way, it keeps your Google apps open when using Google Chrome and uses your proxies through Mozilla Firefox.

Another advantage of social proxies is being able to automate your accounts and divert traffic through them.

Okay VPN seems like a good option; it is a paid (premium) service with quality resident proxies. It costs $20 monthly.

https://www.okayvpn.com

You can choose a few proxies. Then, when creating each fake Facebook profile (according to the nationality of the profile), use an IP proxy from that country. The advantage of Okay VPN is that the resident proxies are already integrated into the VPN (you don't need to configure anything).

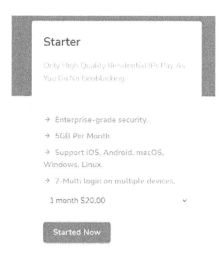

To receive a verification code by SMS, you can use virtual eSIM numbers (no need to have multiple cards or physical smartphones). For this, rent numbers with the 'Numero eSIM' application.

https://www.numeroesim.com

Open several accounts on social media sites like Facebook:

These accounts have previously been confirmed and "prepared." The login information is given.

https://bulkaaccountsale.com

Low prices: 20 Facebook accounts, for example, only cost $14.

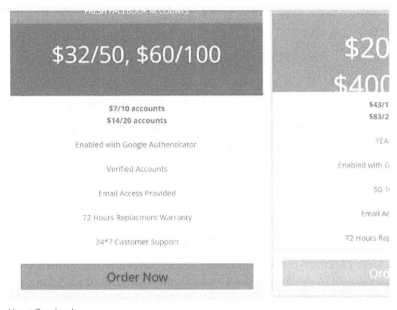

About Facebook

They accept payments made using Perfect Money, Transferwise, Bitcoin, and Visa cards (through Stripe).

https://accountbucks.com

Account Bucks sells Facebook profiles at different prices; for example, 10 accounts for 15 dollars. They also sell Instagram, Gmail, Twitter accounts, etc. They also sell accounts for Twitter, Gmail, and other services. PayPal and Visa are accepted. They also sell followers and likes for all social networks.

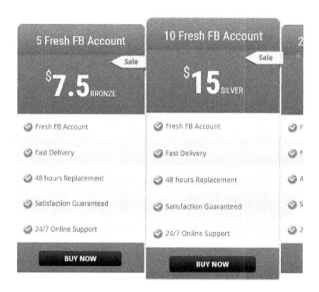

SMM Expert

https://thesmmexpert.com/service/buy-instagram-accounts/

It sells various types of accounts, some four years old, some six years old (aged), from cities in the United States, the United Kingdom, and Europe. The prices begin at $22. Facebook, Instagram, and Gmail accounts, among others. SMS-verified Instagram accounts. Accounts with 5000 followers, accounts with 10,000 followers—there's something for everyone's taste and budget.

You can also buy followers and likes for Twitter, Instagram, Facebook, and other social networks. "Business" Facebook accounts. TripAdvisor reviews. They accept payments by Visa, Skrill, PayPal, and Wepay.

ACC Farm

https://accfarm.com/pt/buy-facebook-accounts

It sells Facebook profiles from different countries for $3.99. Payments can be made with bitcoin, PayPal, and Visa. They also sell gaming and streaming accounts. ACC Farm sells a wide variety of beads. For example, Facebook business accounts, pre-warmed "pre-warmed" accounts. These accounts have already had activity, posts, likes, and engagement for several months.

Another strategy you can use is to buy used, old Instagram accounts (aged accounts) that already have some popularity and thousands of real followers (mostly in the US and UK). Then you will manage these accounts and publish your posts/ads, and products.

One of the websites, for example, is Too Fame:

https://www.toofame.com/shop/page/2/?orderby=price

Prices start at $59 for Instagram accounts with 2000 or 3000 followers. Visa and PayPal are accepted.

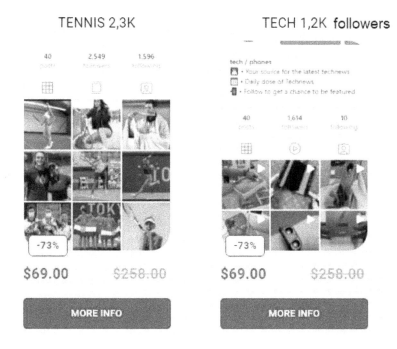

Virtual SIM cards:

To verify accounts via SMS, purchase services from:

https://5sim.net

Instead of owning numerous smartphones and carrier SIM cards, 5SIM allows you to purchase "virtual" cards (which would be expensive).

The SMS code given by social networks to validate the virtual number is automatically received in more than 180 countries.

Numero eSIM

https://www.numeroesim.com

To receive a verification code by SMS, you can use virtual eSIM numbers (no need to have multiple cards or physical smartphones). For this, rent numbers with the Numero eSIM application.

For the typical user, installing these programs and applications is not always straightforward. I merely offer these suggestions out of interest.

The reader can opt for the simple solution of buying followers and likes on the websites I mentioned at the beginning. It is a practical and efficient alternative.

Warming-up accounts

Manage and grow profiles

Tips:

I'm going to offer advice on building and managing profiles, which is referred to as "warming-up."

Imagine that you are managing 10 fake Facebook profiles.

Never log in to all these profiles on the same day.

Save a face photo for later (without ever uploading that photo). This is because Facebook may ask you to verify your identity by uploading a face photo.

Older (aged) profiles are safer, as Facebook already considers them reliable and will not ask for identity verification.

Take for example a female profile, log in using VPN, Proxy and anti-detect browser. Start managing this profile, post some pictures. Manage this profile and post some images. Single-photo profiles inspire "distrust" in both users and the Facebook algorithm, which detects this as fake.

Is it convenient to insert several images of the same person. How do you proceed in this case? Can shop from AI-generated photos or databases (no risk of identity theft).

If you "steal" images from Google Images, you will rarely find multiple photos of the same person. Try stealing from the Web Archive, which has photos from old albums, or from Fotolog, Tumblr, or very old photos (from 2008 or 2009) in which the people don't even look that way today.

If you use old photos of someone from France, from 2008 and put them in a profile from Brazil, it will be very rare for that French person to find out, even more so because they don't even resemble the photos that are more than fifteen years old. It's just a tip.

With this profile, make some interactions: likes, likes, comments, etc. Then logout. Don't use other profiles in a hurry; wait.

Then other day, create another fake profile and administer it.

Don't use all ten fake profiles to "like" the same post or group; this will trigger the algorithm's attention.

Nor should these profiles be your "friends" on your main profile, so there are no links.

Each profile is a different "personality". Don't have the same behavior with all profiles; not everyone can belong to the same football club or like rock music or cats, you know?

For example, in the profile "John" you can behave like a truck driver who loves rock music, smokes, is from the soccer team "Houston Dynamo", etc. You can put posts about football, politics, silly memes, etc.

In a "Anna" profile, you have to act like another persona and like different things, like poetry, promote books, post pictures of perfumes and nail polish, etc.

Do you understand? Also, put common photos that people post: a photo of the puppy, a photo of a meal at a restaurant, a beach, etc.

If the profile simulates, for example, that the girl is from France, search for addresses on Google Maps. Where does she work? Include the name of a local business, the neighborhood in which it is located, the university it attended, and so on. The more specific it is, the more plausible it will be.

Create diversity; not all profiles need to be attractive 30-year-old males or young women; create some older profiles as well (laughs).

Is this ethical? Not totally, but don't do anything illegal (forgeries, phishing, extortion, etc.). As long as you only use these profiles to spread marketing information, likes, and promote books and services, there shouldn't be any malice, right?

Additional advice: Create a female profile with very sensuous photographs if you want a profile that is well-liked and quickly acquires hundreds of friends.

When I created male profiles, it took me a while to gather friends. I sent invitations, but few accepted them.

But with the profile of a sensual woman, I didn't even have to do anything. Hundreds of friend requests poured in, even from strangers (laughs).

I can tell you a secret: as a webmaster, I know that the vast majority of companies of dating websites and applications, such as Meetic, Badoo, Easyflirt, Tinder, etc. They earn millions of dollars, and when they launch an app, they don't start from "zero", because without members, they would never attract men who pay. They start with a database that already contains 50,000 profiles; many of these profiles are purchased from other networks, and many profiles are fake "bots".

Sometimes these bots engage and send sensual messages that resemble a woman seducing or flirting, and the muggle man will pay a monthly fee of $ to read and respond to that message, only to discover that it was a bot! Badoo does this every day!

By the way, I know websites that sell scripts and software to create a dating website, and it already has a database with thousands of women.

eSIM cards

Regarding eSIM (virtual SIM cards or virtual mobile phone numbers), please note that most of these packages offer virtual numbers that expire after 2 weeks or 1 month; they are not permanent numbers. I advise buying inexpensive physical smartphones, those not very sophisticated and disposable ones that cost ten or fifteen dollars, and using SIM cards without loyalty (pre-charged) without contracts so you won't have any charges if you manage a small number of Facebook profiles (10 or 15 accounts). With these inexpensive smartphones and no-contract cards, you may log into Facebook via SMS from accounts. Used smartphones start at $9 on classified online ads, and active SIM cards start at $2.5 as well.

Imagine being able to buy used mobile phones like the "Alcatel 1068" Dual SIM, which allows you to have up to two cards in each mobile phone. If you have five mobile phones (and use two cards in each one), you can use 10 SIM cards with these 5 mobile phones. Now you can receive SMS messages with authentication codes for each Facebook account associated with each profile.

Additionally, as SIM cards are prepaid and come without contracts or monthly fees, you won't have any contract-related costs.

You can place a sticker with the name of the profile on the back of smartphones, for example: Anna's Facebook, John's Facebook, Antonio's Facebook, etc.

To make things simpler, you can connect the smartphones without entering a PIN number into each one of them and leave the cards without a PIN code for the session.

Send bulk messages

In order to distribute your marketing message on Facebook, it is also possible to use a service known as DMS. The letters DM stand for "direct message." Occasionally shortened to Mass DM (Mass Direct Messages).

Some businesses use a bot to accomplish this, but the social network can filter the messages since it views them as "Spam". So on the "black market" there are those who buy these packs of messages, but they will be sent from hundreds of different profiles (the recipients will not even know it was you, nor will your profile appear).

You may have tried to send messages on Facebook Messenger revealing an affiliate link, a link to a blog, or a link to a group of yours, and it was blocked after twenty or thirty messages, correct? Facebook banned you as a spammer, and, in addition, your identity was frowned upon. One option would be to hire a third-party service to do this, right?

On Fiverr, you can find some sellers (from Nigeria, Pakistan, Malaysia, and India) who operate networks of dozens of Facebook profiles and can send these messages with your advertisement. There are packs of 1,000 messages that start at $5. Either through Facebook, as well as by WhatsApp, Telegram or Instagram.

Examples:

https://www.fiverr.com/adesina_5?source=gig_page

https://www.fiverr.com/muhammadzaid396

https://www.fiverr.com/sarahali8

https://www.fiverr.com/asmaawan7345

There are several ways to send massive SMS messages, known as "SMS blasting" or "Bulk SMS". To send your advertisement, you can buy mobile phone numbers on the internet in some forums.

You can also search Google maps, search Facebook profiles, etc. You can use online data scraping tools.

Once you've decided how to send thousands of SMS, you can order them from someone on Fiverr (prices start at $15) or send them using an online service.

But it is necessary to implement the API. The easiest option is to hire someone.

At Fiverr you will find several sellers.

Examples:

https://www.fiverr.com/ayo_awoyemi

The cost of sending 2,000 SMS is approximately $33.

https://www.fiverr.com/kinzahimran

In the Bulk SMS gig, she sells, for example, 5,000 SMS sent for 19 dollars.

https://www.fiverr.com/bilalkhan530

Prices for 500 SMS sent start at $9 from this seller. It also sends massive emails (bulk emails).

https://www.fiverr.com/saied91

This vendor sells email contacts, such as 5,000 emails for $5.

https://www.fiverr.com/cierka_media5

This seller sells email contacts; for exemple, 10,000 verified email addresses, cost $5.

https://www.fiverr.com/dhrubacreator

This seller can create up to 15 Facebook accounts, from the country he wants (then he registers them with the IP of that country). Prices range from $15 to $38.

The Bulk SMS website allows you to send mass messages from several countries; they use numbers in collaboration with several operators.

You can upload the mobile contact list as a CSV, TSV, or XLSX file. It has an online solution (web-based) or desktop application.

Massively send messages to WhatsApp.

There is a solution in the cloud, so it's easy to use and you don't need to download or implement APIs. It's the Send App:

https://sendapp.cloud/

You can send up to 10,000 messages (massively) starting at $19 per month; it contains an autoresponder, a chatbot, automation, etc. In order to create a WhatsApp account, first purchase a virtual number online (do not use your original number to send spam).

To rent a virtual mobile phone number, go to SMS-Man.

https://sms-man.com

Choose your country and the application (such as WhatsApp), and you will receive SMS in your SMS-Man website account. They charge an average of 40 cents per SMS received (that SMS has a PIN code to verify your WhatsApp account).

Let's assume that these SIM cards are linked to the relevant server and enable you to access your account on the website to receive SMS messages rather than a smartphone.

43

Another website is SMS Rent.

https://sms-rent.com/instructions

Join the site by confirming your email after you sign up. then deposit money into the account using PayPal (for example, 5 dollars). Select the nation and SMS provider from which you want to receive messages (example: Portugal and the service is WhatsApp). For an SMS you receive, they charge between €1 and €2, after which you simply confirm the PIN code and use it in the account you made. If you use that code when creating new Facebook accounts, then... Keep in mind to use an anti-detect browser, a proxy, and a VPN with an IP from the target country.

Be warned: avoid sending promotional emails from your personal account. If you do, you risk having your account blocked for breaking the rules, spamming, etc. Send out bulk emails using your another service.

You can sign up for "Send in Blue's" free plan and send up to 300 emails every day. https://www.sendinblue.com

In Send Pulse, in the free account, you can send up to 1500 emails per month.

https://sendpulse.com

Another option is to create a temporary disposable email, which only lasts a few hours, enough to send your spam messages.

https://www.emailondeck.com

Tips for freelance authors

Self publishing

I will continue with black hat techniques, which sharks use.

You like to write books, and you put your first ebook on Amazon. But sales are few, and readers, despite buying a few copies, don't even bother to write a review. What are you going to do? It sits and waits for years, being honest and following Amazon's rules. Or will you buy reviews, as all famous authors do? Do you think all their book reviews were given voluntary and that none were paid for?

If a reader visits your ebook on Amazon and is undecided, and there are no reviews, he will leave. But if it has two or three good reviews saying, "this book is excellent, I loved the content and the way the information was presented, etc.", he will buy it! Furthermore, Amazon gives more prominence to e-books with reviews.

I went to this merchant on Fiverr for reviews in English.

https://www.fiverr.com/theigners

She charges the price of the e-book (as she will have to buy it, and so Amazon considers it a verified purchase and verified review) and then another $25. On average, the service costs $30. This seller posts reviews with different accounts, simulating different people.

Other sellers:

https://www.fiverr.com/aggets

https://www.fiverr.com/bilieiman

Attention: if you want reviews in Portuguese, you can send the text, and they will copy + paste. If you want reviews in English, ask that seller to buy the e-book and write a review on Amazon's American (US) page.

Fiverr sometimes restricts these review accounts. The direct email of "The Igners" is: reviewservice2016@gmail.com

Destroy the competition

Buy dislikes

Another curious and sinister strategy is to buy "dislikes" (not likes) to detonate your competitors.

SMM Buy Sell

https://smmbuysell.com/buy-youtube-dislikes/

For instance, 100 dislikes ($3.50) for videos from a competing channel.

On the other side, SMM Buy Sell offers a range of social media accounts for sale (LinkedIn, Twitter, Facebook, and Instagram). An old LinkedIn account with 300 contacts costs 7.5$. A three-year-old Twitter account with 500 followers costs $18.

Services to grow your YouTube channel: buy likes, comments, shares, hours of views (YouTube now requires a YouTuber to have 4,000 hours of video views to be able to profit from ads), YouTube SEO, and more.

This website has a wide variety of services, like the much-desired reviews for Amazon, for example. Reviews for TripAdvisor, Fiverr, Google Play Store, and other websites.

The Bulk SMM Store website

https://bulksmmstore.com/product/real-100-youtube-dislikes/

For $8, it offers a package of 100 manual "dislikes" (executed by actual people, not bots), and for $10, 1,000 Facebook post "dislikes.".

https://bulksmmstore.com/product/real-1000-facebook-post-likes/

PayPal and Visa are accepted.

They also market other products, such as Facebook video views. views, likes, and subscribers across different social networks. They market web traffic and SEO services. Mirror site
https://buyseostore.com/

These "dislikes" services are also offered by SMM Divine:

https://smmdivine.com/buy-youtube-dislikes

250 YouTube "dislikes" cost $12.5

I'll close with a few more caveats:

Use these methods with caution and only when necessary.

That is, do not rush. Take it easy. Don't buy 5,000 followers or likes right away. Don't acquire followers every month! Your growth has to look "natural".

Buy 300 followers and 150 likes, for example. Then, the following month, buy 100 followers. Then skip shopping for a month. Take steps gradually. Don't use these tools every week or every month, got it?

Avoid sending a lot of friend requests or messages to random people; the Facebook algorithm will flag you as a "spammer" and block your account. Invite five people to friendship, for example, and send six messages. Do the same after a few days.

It's risky to add 20 individuals (friend invites) all at once.

Questions and Answers

Is it common to buy followers and likes?

You will reach your goal in a short time if you buy followers, it is common. That's why many people and businesses buy followers.

Why should I purchase followers?

Buying followers helps you get results more quickly. Since your follower number will be a reference for your project or business development, it also helps you get more organic followers.

Benefits:

Attention is drawn to new posts.

The discussions about your page will be maintained.

Enhancing your social proof.

Increasing the number of followers.

You will improve your credibility.

Getting traffic to your website.

Do hashtags on Instagram bring followers?

Hashtags are great for expanding your social reach. If you have many followers, you can see your posts on the "Explore" page by using appropriate hashtags.

It will help to attract engagement by having a profile with many followers.?

Indeed. It appears that you're a local celebrity when you have many real and active followers on your profile, and people notice this. Because of this, a user who has a lot of followers that are legit will get the attention of potential organic followers.

Why should I buy comments?

When users see that your post has a lot of comments under it, they will be attracted to read your post. It may even end up with getting many more likes since people will visit to see the comments.

What is massliking and massfollowing in Instagram?

Mass liking and mass following in Instagram is a tactic used by marketers to get subscribers quickly. It involves liking or following a large number of accounts over a short period of time, usually within a day. This technique is often used to increase the number of subscribers to a website, but it can also be used to build a loyal audience.

When a user mass likes or follows someone's account, they usually look for hashtags related to the topic or industry of their account to find accounts that might be interested in what they are offering. They then like or follow those accounts in hopes that some of them will reciprocate, and you get more visible.

Instagram lets users make up to 7,500 subscriptions per day, including likes and followers. However, it is recommended that users do not make more than 500-1,000 subscriptions per day to get the best results.

What is the method by which companies deliver comments?

Bots:
Some providers use software or platforms to create, manage and deliver generic comments quickly and in large quantities. While it does its job, the comments are usually obviously fake and the user accounts look fake too.

Comment-for-Comment:
This method is usually part of an exchange network where users perform activities to get the same type of engagement for their own accounts. If your chosen provider has an exchange network, the comments you'll receive are more likely to come from real users.

Rewards:
Companies that use this type of method have their own platform where people perform certain activities to earn points or coins. They can use these points to buy likes, comments, or followers for their own accounts. This method allows you to receive comments from real users.

Promotions:
Some companies create micro-advertising campaigns in order to drive targeted and real engagement to your account. Comments from these promotions are usually high quality and are from real users that have a genuine interest in your posts, but they are usually very expensive and/or not guaranteed.

How Instagram's "Explore" page algorithm Works.

The main purpose of the "Explore" page is to show you new things. Even though Instagram still makes content based on what you might be interested in, most of the posts will come from accounts you don't follow.

In order to determine which posts to rank, the algorithm first looks at posts you have previously interacted with. It then finds out who else has interacted with those posts and what other accounts they're interested in. This will help the Instagram algorithm narrow down which posts will rank for your "Explore" page.

Instagram ranks posts you might be interested in using the following signals after finding a group of posts:

Post information – The popularity of a post is determined by how many likes, comments, and saves it has received. The Explore page weighs much more heavily on these signals than feed and stories.

Interaction history – The post may be from an account you don't follow, but Instagram can tell if you've interacted with their posts before how interested you are in their content.

User activity – The posts you liked, shared, and commented on are considered by Instagram. The history of how you have interacted with other posts on your Explore page is also examined.

Information about the poster – The poster's information is also considered by Instagram, such as how much interaction they have received in the past few weeks. This helps the algorithm find high-quality posts from a wide range of users.

Glossary of terms

Anti-detect browser:
Non-detection browser. It is based on popular browsers, usually Chrome or Firefox. It allows you to create separate browsing environments with your own fingerprint: different browser headers and other identifying information. As a result, sites cannot link these environments to each other. Antidetect browsers are often used to manage multiple accounts on social networks, monitor merchant profiles on e-commerce platforms like Amazon, or run Google Adwords.

Backlinks:
It basically means that "back links" to a specific web resource, also known as inbound links, are hyperlinks from another website to that web resource. If you have a website or blog and you want to rank higher in search engines and have more popularity and traffic, you should have hundreds of links that point to your website; this is achieved with backlinks.

Black Hat:
It defines a more obscure "ethics". The term in the hacker community separates the ethical hackers from the less ethical ones (the black hats), who break the law and lack morals. This distinction was present in 1950s westerns; the phrase "black hats" came about since the evil men typically wore them. Among other things, black hats can represent "obscure" marketing strategies. Black Hat SEO and Black Hat social media are derived terms.

Bot:
Bot, short for robot, also known as an Internet bot or web robot, is a software application designed to mimic human actions repeatedly in a standard way, just as a human would. The algorithms that make up bots are used by Facebook to analyze our posts, classify some as "spam," ban accounts, and other tasks.

Branding:

A set of fundamental solutions for the nutrition and survival of a brand in the market. It encompasses all issues from its formation to its ongoing management, such as its visual identity, positioning strategies, relationship with the public, etc. Short method: create a blog and website; choose the "name" (brand) of the website and domain. Create a logo that represents all of that. Create social networks and promote your brand.

Brandjacking:

It is a harmful action for any company to take its identity online and promote content that could tarnish its image. Brandjackers ensure this kind of behavior by using false profiles. In a sense, you can "detonate" your competitor's brand. "Dislikes" can also be purchased.

Buffer:

Buffer is an online tool for managing social networks that is capable of centralizing all your accounts in one place. Buffer guarantees the visualization of advanced statistics of posts, providing another point of analysis for your social media strategy in addition to allowing you to preset times to upload your posts.

Drip feed:

When we use the term "drip" in relation to social networks, we refer to the slow creation and publication of content (and never all at once). Likes and followers are added gradually (rather than all at once) by websites that offer them, so Facebook or another network is not suspicious. For instance, the customer could purchase 1,000 followers and set up "tasks" to deliver them gradually.

Email bomb:

It's a "email bomb," or perhaps "email bombing" would be a better translation. It is a form of abuse on the network that sends large volumes of emails to an address to overload the mailbox, overload the server.

It can also be a way to send thousands of advertising emails, or spam, using an anonymous and temporary email. Around 20 years ago, infected files (viruses) were also transmitted, the internet was less secure, hacker sites were widely available and simple for the average user (lammer) to access, and they even had the ability to download infected files (in Zip format) and send bomb emails from their own websites.

Farming:
Account farming, for example, means "cultivating" or "creating" various social media accounts, for marketing or other less clear purposes. Make several "Bulk accounts" via bots or software.

Ghost profiles:
They are "ghost" profiles, created by bots or manually by someone, but they only serve to make numbers. These profiles rarely interact.

Guest post:
They are content exchanges between two partners, with each blog publishing content created by the other. This strategy guarantees the strengthening of link building strategies as well as giving both partners greater visibility. Imagine you have a blog and you ask a friend to post about it on their site with a link back to yours. You'll follow suit. There are paid solutions available where you may hire a well-known blogger to create a blog post promoting your book or product about you.

Hashtag:
The hashtag symbol is #. (pound sign). It is used to highlight terms that are pertinent in a particular context and index them in social media search directories like Twitter, Facebook, Google+, and Instagram, for instance, in the form of a hyperlink or shortcut to the marked material. In English, "tag" means "to mark" or "to mark," and "hash" is the cardinal symbol itself.

Influencer:

A user with a large social network following and the ability to influence the purchasing decisions or interactions of other common users.

Like:

Thumb up, is a way to let people know that you enjoy it without leaving a comment.

Marketing automation:

Marketing automation refers to the use of tools that aim to automate your digital marketing processes, making the management process more organized, agile, and scalable. It can be used in conjunction with email marketing, for example, and for some social networks, it can be incorporated to help schedule posts and organize an editorial calendar.

Meme:

Memes in social networks are regularly shared by users in a viral fashion and include pictures, expressions, prints, movies, gifs, etc. Images of Gretchen, Leonardo DiCaprio with the Oscar, or The Shining with witty comments are a few examples that are frequently used.

PBNs:

Webrings, or Private Blog Networks, are groups of websites and blogs that connect to each other with hyperlinks. They are designed to build domain authority and increase each website's ranking on Google. I think it's a necessary evil, because nowadays it's hard to make link partnerships with other bloggers; they're too stupid, selfish, and self-centered and refuse to exchange links and traffic with similar blogs (because they're afraid of competition), anyway.
So the most practical method is for you to create several blogs in different places (Blogger, Wordpress, sites on Wix, on Weebly, etc.) with content and posts, then in the partner links you will place links to

your other websites. The traffic exchange is done between several of your blogs in an "internal network", you know? I don't see any harm as long as the blogs have diverse and different content (they cannot be clones of each other with the same content).
Imagine that you have a "Blog A", the visitor goes to your "Blog B", then "Blog C", "Blog D", but all the blogs have a different look and content and themes, there is quality content.

What do you prefer? Ask a half-dozen bloggers for links who will likely decline, or pay for ads and web traffic, spending hundreds of dollars? Or do you prefer to gradually build your own network of blogs and websites year after year?

I have about 11 websites and 16 blogs, and if I count the monthly visits to all of them, the number reaches 4 million.

Phishing:
A dishonest attempt to gain private information such as logins, passwords, and credit card numbers by imitating the designs of reputable organizations, typically through emails. The term, a technological version of "fishing," was created by hackers who stole America Online (AOL) user accounts and passwords in 1996.

Pins:
Pins are equivalent to social media "favorites". On Pinterest, a user can "pin" any online content he wants, placing it in virtual folders for later consultation.

Post:
A post is content created and published on some internet platform. This material may be presented as text, audio, video, images, or a combination of all of them...In English, "post" or "to post" means "to publish".

Pre-warmed accounts:
"Pre-warmed" accounts are pre-warmed. These accounts have

already had activity, posts, likes, and engagement for several months. There are also old "aged accounts" for sale. Consider how much more superior and delicious a 12-year-old whiskey is compared to an 8-year-old whiskey. Old accounts from Facebook (or other social networks) are more valuable on the open market.

Proxy:
A proxy is a form of gateway between web servers and an internet-connected device. Web requests made from the device must go through the proxy to this provided intermediary before reaching the target web page server (such as Facebook). Before reaching the device, the results of the requested page first go to the proxy server, so your IP is never seen, only the proxy IP.

ROI (Return on Investment):
It is a metric widely used in social media management and indicates how much financial return there was after the acquisition of a certain investment (both for tools and for infrastructure). It is possible to calculate the conversion of leads from paid advertisements on social networks, such as Facebook.

SMM panel:
The Social Media Marketing Panel is a website that has strategies to attract segmented followers to an Instagram, Facebook, or other network profile, increasing its visibility and engagement.

SEO:
Search Engine Optimization encompasses a series of practices to increase the organic visualization of a page or its content through search engines such as Google. It focuses on optimizing content formatting and the use of keywords, in addition to understanding the main ranking rules of search engines.

Troll:

Malicious user with the sole purpose of generating online conflicts and controversies. It gave rise to the expression "don't feed the troll", indicating the need to avoid this type of user and not give them rope for the conflicts they initiate.

Viral:

Term used to describe any text, image, or piece of content that spreads quickly over the internet (generally due to the high share rate), generating an exponential increase in visits when compared to normal business access rates.

VPN:

Initials for a virtual private network. It is a service or tool that safeguards your online privacy and connection to the internet.
You can browse using an IP address from any nation while disguising your home country's IP. On the internet, there are some free browser add-ons and programs.

Bibliography

I have already mentioned the sources with all the links, but also consulted Wikipedia.

My other titles:

"Vrajitoare - Gypsy Magick".

"Black Magick Rituals".

"Obscure Dimensions and Magickal Systems".

"Vampyros Magicae – Real Vampyre Magick".

"Binding and Domination Spells".

"Magickal Formulary - 620 Spells".

"Narcos Magick"

"Santa Muerte Codex"

https://www.occult-books.com

https://www.macumba-school.com

https://www.instagram.com/asamod777/

https://www.tiktok.com/@macumbaschool

https://www.youtube.com/@asamod777

www.ingramcontent.com/pod-product-compliance
Lightning Source LLC
Chambersburg PA
CBHW070857070326
40690CB00009B/1889